Intelligence Agencies' Role in the 1983 U.S. Military Intervention in Grenada

Copyright Page

TITLE: Intelligence Agencies' Role in the 1983 U.S. Military Intervention in Grenada

1ST Edition

Copyright @ 2023

ISBN: 9798223320753

Table of Contents

Intelligence Agencies' Role in the 1983 U.S. Military Intervention in Grenada

By Roberto Miguel Rodriguez

Chapter 1: The 1983 U.S. Military Intervention in Grenada

Background of Grenada prior to the intervention

Before delving into the details of the 1983 U.S. military intervention in Grenada, it is essential to understand the historical and political context of the Caribbean nation. Grenada, an island country located in the eastern Caribbean Sea, had a complex background that played a significant role in shaping the events leading up to the intervention.

Grenada gained independence from British colonial rule on February 7, 1974, under the leadership of Prime Minister Eric Gairy. However, Gairy's rule was marked by allegations of corruption, human rights abuses, and political repression, which created an atmosphere of discontent among the population. In 1979, a Marxist-Leninist revolutionary group called the New Jewel Movement (NJM) led by Maurice Bishop seized power in a bloodless coup, overthrowing Gairy's government.

Under Bishop's leadership, Grenada embarked on a path of socialist revolution, aligning itself with Cuba and the Soviet Union. The NJM implemented policies that aimed to redistribute wealth, improve social services, and strengthen ties with other socialist nations. Despite some positive reforms, Bishop's regime faced internal divisions and economic challenges, leading to growing dissent within the party and among Grenadian citizens.

In October 1983, a power struggle within the NJM culminated in the house arrest and subsequent execution of Maurice Bishop by a faction led by Deputy Prime Minister Bernard Coard. This event triggered a series of protests and demonstrations by the population demanding democratic reforms and the restoration of Bishop's government.

Concerned about the potential for increased Soviet influence in the region and fearing the establishment of a communist regime in Grenada, the United States viewed these developments as a threat to its national security interests. The Reagan administration, already engaged in the Cold War against the Soviet Union, decided to intervene militarily in Grenada to restore order and protect American citizens on the island.

The U.S. military intervention, code-named Operation Urgent Fury, began on October 25, 1983. It involved a joint force of U.S. Marines, Army Rangers, and special operations units, supported by troops from several Caribbean nations. The intervention resulted in the successful removal of the Coard-led military junta and the restoration of democratic governance in Grenada.

The aftermath of the intervention witnessed a period of political instability and economic challenges for Grenada. The country faced difficulties in rebuilding its infrastructure and recovering from the trauma of the intervention. Additionally, the intervention had significant diplomatic repercussions, straining U.S.-Caribbean relations and raising questions about the legality of the military action under international law.

In conclusion, understanding the background of Grenada prior to the intervention is crucial for comprehending the complexities and implications of the 1983 U.S. military intervention. It sets the stage for exploring the political, diplomatic, military, and humanitarian aspects of this historic event and its impact on Grenada and the wider Caribbean region.

Motivations behind the U.S. decision to intervene in Grenada

The 1983 U.S. Military Intervention in Grenada remains one of the most controversial events in the history of U.S. foreign policy. To fully understand the motivations behind this decision, it is important to examine the geopolitical and strategic factors that influenced the United States to intervene in the small Caribbean nation.

One of the key motivations for the U.S. intervention in Grenada was the concern over the growing influence of communist forces in the region. In the early 1980s, the Soviet Union and Cuba were providing military and economic support to the Grenadian government, which had recently undergone a coup. This raised fears in Washington that Grenada could become a communist stronghold and pose a threat to U.S. interests in the Caribbean.

Additionally, the U.S. government had concerns about the safety of its citizens on the island. After the coup in Grenada, there were reports of violence and human rights abuses, including the imprisonment of political opponents. The Reagan administration argued that the intervention was necessary to protect American students studying at the St. George's University, who were at risk of becoming hostages.

Furthermore, the intervention in Grenada was seen as an opportunity for the United States to assert its dominance in the region and send a message to other nations about its willingness to use military force to protect its interests. This was particularly important in the context of the Cold War, where the United States sought to contain the spread of communism and maintain its position as a global superpower.

Another motivation behind the U.S. decision to intervene in Grenada was the desire to demonstrate solidarity with its allies in the region. Several Caribbean nations, including Jamaica and Barbados, had expressed concerns about the situation in Grenada and called for international action. The United States, therefore, saw the intervention as an opportunity to strengthen its relationships with these countries and maintain its influence in the region.

In conclusion, the motivations behind the U.S. decision to intervene in Grenada were multifaceted. They included concerns about the spread of communism, the safety of American citizens, the desire to assert dominance in the region, and the need to maintain strong alliances with Caribbean nations. To fully understand the consequences and implications of the intervention, it is crucial to consider these motivations within the broader context of Cold War politics and U.S. foreign policy objectives.

Planning and preparation for the military intervention

The planning and preparation for the 1983 U.S. military intervention in Grenada were complex and multifaceted. This subchapter explores the various aspects that intelligence agencies played in the planning process, as well as the political implications, military strategies, and humanitarian aspects of the intervention.

Intelligence agencies, such as the Central Intelligence Agency (CIA) and the Defense Intelligence Agency (DIA), played a critical role in gathering and analyzing information about the political and military situation in Grenada. Their assessments of the threat posed by the Marxist government of Maurice Bishop and its ties to Cuba and the Soviet Union were instrumental in shaping the decision to intervene. Through covert operations, they infiltrated Grenada to gather intelligence on the island's military capabilities, infrastructure, and political dynamics.

The planning process involved collaboration between various government agencies, including the Department of Defense and the National Security Council. Their aim was to develop a comprehensive strategy that would ensure the success of the intervention while minimizing casualties and civilian harm. Military strategies, such as the use of Special Operations Forces and a joint task force, were employed to achieve these objectives.

The political implications of the intervention were significant. The United States justified its actions as a response to the threat posed by the Marxist government in Grenada to regional stability and U.S. national security interests. However, the intervention faced criticism from the international community, particularly from countries in the Caribbean and the Non-Aligned Movement, who saw it as a violation of international law and an infringement on Grenada's sovereignty.

The media coverage of the intervention played a crucial role in shaping public opinion. Journalists were embedded with the U.S. forces and provided real-time updates on the progress of the operation. However, there were limitations on their access, and some aspects of the intervention were kept classified. This led to debates about the accuracy and objectivity of the media coverage.

The humanitarian aspects of the intervention focused on providing medical assistance, restoring infrastructure, and establishing democratic governance in Grenada. The U.S. government sought to win the hearts and minds of the Grenadian people by delivering aid and promoting stability and development.

The diplomatic repercussions of the intervention were far-reaching. It strained U.S.-Caribbean relations, as many Caribbean countries viewed the intervention as a violation of their regional sovereignty. Additionally, the intervention prompted a reassessment of the collective security arrangements in the Caribbean, leading to the establishment of the Caribbean Community (CARICOM) and the Caribbean Basin Initiative.

In conclusion, the planning and preparation for the 1983 U.S. military intervention in Grenada involved intelligence agencies, political considerations, military strategies, and humanitarian efforts. The intervention had significant consequences for regional stability, international law, U.S.-Caribbean relations, and the media coverage of military operations. Understanding these aspects is crucial for historians and those interested in the 1983 U.S. military intervention in Grenada and its aftermath.

Chapter 2: The Aftermath of the 1983 U.S. Military Intervention in Grenada

Immediate consequences and impact on the Grenadian population

The immediate consequences and impact of the 1983 U.S. military intervention in Grenada had profound effects on the Grenadian population. This subchapter explores the various ways in which the intervention shaped the lives of the people of Grenada and the lasting implications it had on their society.

First and foremost, the military intervention resulted in a significant loss of life among the Grenadian population. The initial assault by U.S. forces led to the deaths of numerous Grenadian soldiers and civilians, many of whom were caught in the crossfire. The violence and destruction caused by the intervention left families grieving and communities devastated.

In addition to the loss of life, the intervention had severe economic consequences for Grenada. The country's infrastructure, including roads, bridges, and buildings, suffered extensive damage during the military operations. The already fragile economy of Grenada was further weakened, leading to a deepening of poverty and unemployment among the population.

The intervention also had implications for the political landscape of Grenada. The U.S. invasion resulted in the removal of the Marxist-led People's Revolutionary Government (PRG) and the restoration of a democratic system. While some hailed this as a positive development, others questioned the legitimacy of the intervention and its impact on Grenada's sovereignty.

Furthermore, the intervention had a lasting impact on regional stability. The U.S. military action in Grenada raised concerns among neighboring

Caribbean nations about the potential for future interventions in the region. It also highlighted the power dynamics between the United States and its smaller Caribbean neighbors, leading to a reassessment of their relationships.

The humanitarian aspects of the intervention cannot be overlooked. While the U.S. claimed its intervention was for humanitarian purposes, there were reports of human rights abuses committed by both sides during the conflict. The Grenadian population faced challenges in accessing basic necessities such as food, water, and medical supplies, further exacerbating the already dire conditions.

Lastly, the diplomatic repercussions of the intervention were significant. The United States faced criticism from various countries and international organizations for its unilateral action. The intervention strained diplomatic relations between the United States and other nations, particularly those in the Caribbean region.

In conclusion, the immediate consequences and impact of the 1983 U.S. military intervention in Grenada were far-reaching and multifaceted. The loss of life, economic devastation, political implications, and diplomatic repercussions all had a profound effect on the Grenadian population. The intervention not only reshaped the lives of individuals but also had lasting implications for the region and U.S.-Caribbean relations.

Rebuilding efforts and restoration of stability in Grenada

Following the 1983 U.S. military intervention in Grenada, the small Caribbean island faced significant challenges in rebuilding its infrastructure and restoring stability. This subchapter explores the efforts that were made to address these issues and the long-term consequences of the intervention.

In the aftermath of the military intervention, the United States, along with other international actors, played a crucial role in providing aid and support for Grenada's reconstruction. The focus was on restoring essential services such as electricity, water, and healthcare, which had been severely disrupted during the conflict. International organizations like the United Nations and the Organization of American States also contributed to these efforts, mobilizing resources and expertise to assist in the rebuilding process.

The political implications of the intervention were far-reaching. The United States, by overthrowing the Marxist government of Maurice Bishop, sought to establish a more democratic and stable regime in Grenada. However, the intervention was met with mixed reactions. While some viewed it as a necessary action to prevent the spread of communism in the region, others criticized it as a violation of international law and an infringement on Grenada's sovereignty.

The impact of the intervention on regional stability was also a significant concern. The United States aimed to restore stability not only in Grenada but also in the wider Caribbean region. By removing a potential threat to neighboring countries, such as Trinidad and Tobago and Barbados, the intervention sought to prevent the destabilization of the entire region.

The media coverage of the intervention played a crucial role in shaping public opinion. While the U.S. government sought to control the narrative and present the intervention as a necessary and successful mission, there were controversies and debates surrounding the media's access to information and the portrayal of events on the ground.

The military strategies employed during the intervention were highly effective in achieving the primary objective of removing the Grenadian government and rescuing U.S. citizens. However, there were concerns about the level of force used and the potential for civilian casualties.

From a humanitarian perspective, the intervention had both positive and negative consequences. While it restored essential services and brought stability to Grenada, there were reports of human rights abuses and violations during the military operation.

The diplomatic repercussions of the intervention were felt not only in Grenada but also in the wider international community. The United States faced criticism from countries that viewed the intervention as an act of aggression and a breach of international law. The intervention also strained U.S.-Caribbean relations, with some countries expressing resentment towards U.S. interventionism in the region.

Finally, this subchapter highlights the role of intelligence agencies in planning the intervention. It explores the intelligence gathering and analysis that led to the decision to intervene in Grenada and the lessons learned from this experience.

Overall, the rebuilding efforts and restoration of stability in Grenada following the 1983 U.S. military intervention had a lasting impact on the country and the wider region. While the intervention achieved its immediate objectives, it also raised important questions about the role of international law, the use of force, and the long-term consequences of military interventions.

Long-term effects on Grenada's political and social landscape

The 1983 U.S. military intervention in Grenada had profound and lasting effects on the political and social landscape of the country. These effects continue to shape Grenada's development and its relationship with the international community.

From a political standpoint, the intervention led to a significant shift in power dynamics within Grenada. The invasion effectively toppled the Marxist government of Prime Minister Maurice Bishop and the People's Revolutionary Government (PRG). This led to a period of political uncertainty and instability, as various factions vied for control of the country. Eventually, a democratic government was restored, but the political landscape remained fragmented, with deep divisions between supporters of the former PRG and those who favored a more conservative approach.

The intervention also had a profound social impact on Grenada. The country's infrastructure was severely damaged during the invasion, with key buildings and facilities destroyed. This created significant challenges for the government in terms of rebuilding and providing basic services to the population. Furthermore, the invasion disrupted the social fabric of the country, leading to a breakdown in trust and cohesion among the population.

In the aftermath of the intervention, Grenada's economy struggled to recover. The country heavily relied on tourism and agriculture, both of which were severely impacted by the invasion. The destruction of infrastructure, coupled with the loss of international investment, hindered economic growth and development. Grenada's economy has since made strides towards recovery, but the intervention had long-lasting consequences on the country's economic stability.

The intervention also had wider implications for regional stability. Grenada's proximity to other Caribbean nations raised concerns among neighboring countries about the potential for military intervention in their own territories. This led to increased tensions and a sense of vulnerability among regional nations.

On an international scale, the intervention sparked debates about the role of international law and the use of force in resolving conflicts. The United States' unilateral decision to intervene without a mandate from the United Nations raised questions about the limits of state sovereignty and the responsibility of powerful nations in global affairs.

The media coverage of the intervention also played a significant role in shaping public perception and understanding of the events in Grenada. The media's portrayal of the intervention and its aftermath influenced public opinion and contributed to the narrative surrounding the intervention.

The long-term effects of the intervention on U.S.-Caribbean relations were also significant. The invasion strained diplomatic ties between the United States and Caribbean nations, as many viewed the intervention as an infringement on their sovereignty. It took time for trust to be rebuilt and for relations to normalize.

In conclusion, the 1983 U.S. military intervention in Grenada had far-reaching and enduring effects on the country's political and social landscape. It fundamentally altered power dynamics, disrupted social cohesion, and hindered economic development. The intervention also had wider implications for regional stability, international law, media coverage, and U.S.-Caribbean relations. Understanding these long-term effects is crucial for historians and those interested in studying the aftermath of the intervention and its consequences on Grenada and the wider world.

Chapter 3: The Political Implications of the 1983 U.S. Military Intervention in Grenada

Changes in the Grenadian government and political system

The 1983 U.S. military intervention in Grenada marked a turning point in the country's government and political system. Prior to the intervention, Grenada had been under the rule of the People's Revolutionary Government (PRG), a Marxist-Leninist regime led by Prime Minister Maurice Bishop. However, internal conflicts within the PRG led to a power struggle, resulting in Bishop's execution and the subsequent collapse of the government.

Following the intervention, the U.S. military established a new interim government, known as the National Joint Consultative Council (NJCC), to restore stability and oversee the transition to democratic rule. The NJCC comprised representatives from various political factions and civil society groups, aiming to foster a more inclusive and representative political system. This marked a significant departure from the previous authoritarian regime, as the NJCC allowed for greater participation and representation of different political ideologies.

In the aftermath of the intervention, Grenada underwent a series of political reforms. A new constitution was drafted, laying the foundation for a democratic system. Elections were held in 1984, resulting in the victory of the New National Party (NNP), led by Herbert Blaize. Blaize's government implemented market-oriented economic policies and pursued closer ties with the United States and other Western powers.

The political implications of the intervention were far-reaching. It sparked debates on the legitimacy of foreign military interventions and raised questions about sovereignty and self-determination. While some historians argue that the intervention was necessary to prevent the establishment of a communist regime in Grenada and protect regional stability, others criticize it as a violation of international law and an infringement on Grenada's sovereignty.

The intervention also had a significant impact on regional stability. It sent a clear message to other Caribbean nations that the United States was willing to use military force to protect its interests in the region. This had both positive and negative consequences, as it deterred potential threats to U.S. interests but also raised concerns about American imperialism and interventionism.

The media coverage of the intervention played a crucial role in shaping public opinion and perceptions of the event. The U.S. government carefully managed the narrative, emphasizing the need to protect American citizens and restore democracy in Grenada. However, critics argue that the media coverage was biased and failed to provide a comprehensive understanding of the complex political dynamics at play.

From a military perspective, the intervention showcased the effectiveness of rapid deployment and joint military operations. The U.S. forces employed innovative tactics and strategies, such as the use of airborne assault and special operations forces, to achieve their objectives swiftly and minimize casualties.

The humanitarian aspects of the intervention cannot be overlooked. The U.S. military provided medical assistance, restored essential services, and facilitated the delivery of humanitarian aid to the Grenadian population. These efforts were crucial in restoring stability and rebuilding the country after years of political turmoil.

Diplomatically, the intervention strained relations between the United States and several Caribbean nations, who saw it as an infringement on Grenada's sovereignty and a threat to regional stability. It took years for these relationships to mend, and the intervention continues to be a sensitive issue in U.S.-Caribbean relations.

In conclusion, the 1983 U.S. military intervention in Grenada brought about significant changes in the country's government and political system. It led to the collapse of the Marxist-Leninist regime and the establishment of a more inclusive and representative interim government. The intervention had wide-ranging implications, including debates on sovereignty and self-determination, impacts on regional stability and U.S.-Caribbean relations, and military and humanitarian aspects. Understanding these changes is crucial to comprehending the complex consequences of this historical event.

Regional reactions and responses to the intervention

The 1983 U.S. military intervention in Grenada sent shockwaves throughout the region, triggering a wide range of reactions and responses from neighboring countries and regional organizations. This subchapter delves into the regional perspectives on the intervention, exploring its impact on regional stability, diplomatic relations, and the political landscape of the Caribbean.

Immediately following the intervention, the reaction from the Caribbean nations was mixed. While some governments, such as Jamaica and Dominica, expressed support for the U.S. action, others, including Barbados and Trinidad and Tobago, voiced strong opposition. These varying responses reflected the deep divisions within the region, with some countries perceiving the intervention as a necessary measure to restore democracy in Grenada, while others saw it as a blatant violation of sovereignty.

The aftermath of the intervention witnessed a significant shift in regional politics. Several Caribbean nations, previously aligned with socialist ideologies, began to distance themselves from leftist governments, fearing similar interventions in their own countries. The U.S. intervention served as a stark reminder of the potential consequences of challenging American interests in the region, leading to a realignment of political alliances and a strengthening of ties with the United States.

Regional stability also became a major concern in the wake of the intervention. The abrupt military action had created a power vacuum in Grenada, which raised concerns about the potential for further instability and violence. Caribbean governments and regional organizations, such as the Organization of Eastern Caribbean States (OECS) and the Caribbean Community (CARICOM), played crucial roles in facilitating the transition to democracy in Grenada and ensuring regional stability.

Furthermore, the intervention had significant diplomatic repercussions for U.S.-Caribbean relations. The unilateral nature of the intervention strained diplomatic ties between the United States and some Caribbean nations, resulting in a period of distrust and tension. However, over time, efforts were made to repair these relationships through increased diplomatic engagement and aid programs, which aimed to rebuild trust and foster cooperation in areas such as security and economic development.

Historians examining the 1983 U.S. military intervention in Grenada must take into account the diverse regional reactions and responses to fully grasp its impact. The intervention had far-reaching consequences on regional stability, political dynamics, and diplomatic relations within the Caribbean. It reshaped the regional landscape, prompting a reassessment of political ideologies, alliances, and the role of external powers in Caribbean affairs. The reactions and responses from neighboring countries provide valuable insights into the multifaceted nature of this historic event and its lasting effects on the region.

Influence on U.S. foreign policy in the Caribbean

The influence of U.S. foreign policy in the Caribbean region cannot be understated, particularly in relation to the 1983 military intervention in Grenada. This subchapter delves into the various factors that shaped U.S. decision-making and their consequent impact on the region.

Historically, the United States has viewed the Caribbean as its sphere of influence, with strategic and economic interests at stake. Throughout the Cold War era, the Caribbean became a battleground for ideological supremacy between the United States and the Soviet Union. This rivalry intensified in the early 1980s, leading to the U.S. assessment that Grenada posed a threat to regional stability and U.S. interests.

The aftermath of the 1983 military intervention in Grenada witnessed significant political implications. The U.S.-backed government installed after the intervention faced challenges in establishing legitimacy and facing accusations of neo-colonialism. This event also raised concerns among regional governments about potential U.S. interference in their internal affairs, thus reshaping the dynamics of U.S.-Caribbean relations.

The impact of the intervention on regional stability was multifaceted. While the U.S. intervention successfully removed a perceived communist threat in Grenada, it also raised concerns about the potential for future military interventions in the region. The United States had to navigate these concerns to maintain its influence in the Caribbean and ensure regional stability.

International law played a crucial role in shaping the U.S. military intervention in Grenada. The United States justified its actions based on the principle of self-defense and the need to protect American citizens. However, critics argued that the intervention violated the sovereignty of a sovereign nation and challenged the legitimacy of such actions under international law.

The media coverage surrounding the military intervention in Grenada was significant and had both positive and negative implications. The U.S. government actively managed the narrative, emphasizing the need for intervention to protect American lives and restore democracy. However, media scrutiny also exposed inconsistencies in the government's justifications and raised questions about the true motivations behind the intervention.

The military strategies employed during the intervention were a combination of rapid deployment, overwhelming force, and coordination between various branches of the military. The success of these strategies in achieving the stated objectives of the intervention was evident. However, critics argue that the use of force was disproportionate and resulted in civilian casualties.

The humanitarian aspects of the intervention cannot be overlooked. The U.S. military provided aid and assistance to the Grenadian people, including medical care, food, and infrastructure rebuilding. However, some critics argue that the humanitarian efforts were overshadowed by the perception that the intervention was driven by political and strategic motives.

Diplomatically, the intervention strained U.S.-Caribbean relations. Regional governments expressed concerns about the violation of sovereignty and the potential for future interventions. The United States had to navigate these diplomatic repercussions and work towards rebuilding trust and cooperation with Caribbean nations.

The role of intelligence agencies in planning the intervention was crucial. The CIA and other intelligence agencies provided information and analysis that informed U.S. decision-making. However, questions were raised about the accuracy of intelligence assessments and the potential for intelligence failures.

Overall, the 1983 U.S. military intervention in Grenada had far-reaching implications for U.S.-Caribbean relations, regional stability, and the role of international law in military interventions. This subchapter aims to provide a comprehensive understanding of the influence of U.S. foreign policy in the Caribbean and shed light on the complexities surrounding the intervention and its aftermath.

Chapter 4: The Impact of the 1983 U.S. Military Intervention in Grenada on Regional Stability

Relationship between Grenada and neighboring countries post-intervention

The relationship between Grenada and its neighboring countries underwent significant changes in the aftermath of the 1983 U.S. military intervention. The intervention, which aimed to restore order and democracy in Grenada following a coup, had wide-ranging political implications not only for Grenada but also for the surrounding region.

One of the immediate consequences of the intervention was the strained relations between Grenada and its Caribbean neighbors. Several countries in the region, such as Barbados and Jamaica, had expressed concerns about the U.S. military action, viewing it as a violation of international law and an infringement on Grenada's sovereignty. These tensions led to a period of diplomatic isolation for Grenada within the Caribbean community.

However, over time, the relationship between Grenada and its neighbors began to improve. The U.S.-Caribbean relations, which had been strained due to the intervention, gradually started to normalize. The United States made efforts to rebuild diplomatic ties with the Caribbean nations and provide assistance for the reconstruction and development of Grenada.

The impact of the intervention on regional stability was a topic of much debate. While some argued that the intervention had brought stability to Grenada and prevented the establishment of a Soviet-aligned government, others contended that it had destabilized the region by setting a precedent for foreign military intervention in Caribbean affairs.

This debate influenced the relationship between Grenada and its neighbors, as some countries remained skeptical of U.S. intentions in the region.

The media coverage of the intervention played a crucial role in shaping public opinion and the perception of Grenada's neighbors. The media portrayed the intervention as a necessary measure to protect American lives and restore democracy in Grenada. This coverage, coupled with the U.S. government's efforts to address concerns and rebuild relations, contributed to a gradual improvement in the perception of the intervention among Grenada's neighbors.

Overall, the relationship between Grenada and its neighboring countries post-intervention was characterized by initial tensions and diplomatic isolation, followed by a gradual improvement in relations. The intervention had significant political implications for Grenada and the region, raising questions about international law, regional stability, and foreign military interventions. The role of intelligence agencies in planning the intervention and the humanitarian aspects of the operation also shaped the post-intervention relationship between Grenada and its neighbors. The impact of the intervention on U.S.-Caribbean relations, in particular, underscored the complexities of regional dynamics and the challenges of balancing sovereignty and external intervention in the Caribbean context.

Regional security concerns and implications for Caribbean nations

The 1983 U.S. military intervention in Grenada had significant regional security concerns and implications for Caribbean nations. This subchapter explores the various aspects of these concerns and their impact on the region.

One of the most immediate concerns was the potential destabilization of the Caribbean region as a result of the intervention. The sudden military action by the United States raised fears among neighboring countries about their own security. They were uncertain about the intentions of the U.S. and whether similar interventions could occur in their territories. This fear was further exacerbated by the lack of consultation or prior warning given to the Caribbean nations.

Another concern was the potential for a power vacuum in Grenada itself. With the removal of the Marxist government and the establishment of a U.S.-backed administration, there were fears that internal conflicts could arise. The neighboring countries were concerned about the impact of such conflicts on their own stability and security.

Furthermore, the intervention brought to the forefront the issue of sovereignty and the role of international law in the region. Many Caribbean nations questioned the legality of the U.S. military action and the violation of Grenada's sovereignty. This raised concerns about the vulnerability of smaller nations to external intervention and the need for stronger adherence to international law.

The diplomatic repercussions of the intervention were also significant. The Caribbean nations, as a collective, voiced their opposition to the intervention and condemned the United States for its actions. This strained diplomatic relations between the U.S. and the Caribbean nations, leading to a period of tension and mistrust.

Additionally, the intervention had a lasting impact on U.S.-Caribbean relations. The unilateral action by the U.S. without consultation or consideration for the concerns of the Caribbean nations created a sense of resentment and mistrust. This strained relationship affected various aspects of cooperation, including trade, security, and regional integration.

In conclusion, the 1983 U.S. military intervention in Grenada had far-reaching regional security concerns and implications for Caribbean nations. The intervention raised fears of destabilization, questioned the principles of sovereignty and international law, strained diplomatic relations, and impacted U.S.-Caribbean relations. These concerns and implications continue to shape the region's approach to security and cooperation to this day.

Influence on regional cooperation and alliances

The 1983 U.S. military intervention in Grenada had a significant impact on regional cooperation and alliances in the Caribbean and beyond. This subchapter will explore the various ways in which the intervention shaped the political landscape and influenced regional stability in the aftermath of the operation.

One of the immediate consequences of the intervention was the strain it placed on regional alliances. The Organization of Eastern Caribbean States (OECS), which had been established to promote cooperation and mutual defense among its member countries, faced a dilemma when the United States invaded Grenada without consulting or seeking approval from the organization. This unilateral action by the U.S. caused divisions within the OECS and raised questions about the effectiveness and legitimacy of regional alliances.

Furthermore, the intervention had a chilling effect on the relationship between the United States and other Caribbean countries. Many nations in the region viewed the invasion as a violation of sovereignty and a threat to their own independence. This led to increased tensions and mistrust between the U.S. and its Caribbean neighbors, straining diplomatic relations and hindering future cooperation.

The intervention also had implications for the wider international community and its perception of U.S. military actions. The invasion of Grenada was widely condemned by the United Nations General Assembly, with many countries expressing concern over the disregard for international law and the precedent it set for unilateral military interventions. This criticism further isolated the United States and eroded its credibility as a global leader.

In terms of regional stability, the intervention had mixed results. While it initially restored order and removed a perceived threat to the region, it also created a power vacuum and left a void in Grenada's political leadership. This instability had ripple effects across the Caribbean, as neighboring countries grappled with the consequences of the intervention and the potential for further military interventions in the future.

In conclusion, the 1983 U.S. military intervention in Grenada had far-reaching implications for regional cooperation and alliances. It strained relationships between the United States and its Caribbean neighbors, raised doubts about the effectiveness of regional alliances, and sparked international criticism of U.S. military actions. The intervention also created instability in Grenada and the wider region, leaving a lasting impact on the political landscape of the Caribbean.

Chapter 5: The Role of International Law in the 1983 U.S. Military Intervention in Grenada

Legality and justifications for the intervention under international law

The 1983 U.S. military intervention in Grenada sparked intense debate regarding its legality under international law. This subchapter aims to analyze the legal justifications put forth by the United States and examine the implications of these justifications.

The U.S. government argued that the military intervention in Grenada was justified under the principles of self-defense and collective security. The deteriorating political situation in Grenada, marked by a coup and the establishment of a Marxist-Leninist government, raised concerns about the safety of American citizens and regional stability. The U.S. invoked Article 51 of the United Nations Charter, which allows for self-defense in response to an armed attack, to justify its intervention. Furthermore, invoking the Organization of American States' (OAS) collective security principle, the U.S. claimed it had a duty to protect the region from the spread of communism.

Critics, however, argued that the U.S. intervention violated international law. They contended that Grenada did not pose a direct threat to the United States, and therefore, the principle of self-defense did not apply. Additionally, they questioned the legitimacy of the OAS collective security principle, arguing that it was merely a cover for U.S. interventionism in the region.

The legality of the intervention was further complicated by the absence of a United Nations Security Council resolution authorizing the use of force. Some historians argue that the U.S. bypassed the Security Council due to concerns about potential opposition from Soviet allies, such as

Cuba. This raised questions about the U.S. commitment to the rule of law and respect for international institutions.

The consequences of the U.S. intervention in Grenada extended beyond legal debates. It had profound political implications, both domestically and internationally. Domestically, the intervention was initially popular, boosting President Reagan's approval ratings. However, it later became a subject of controversy, with critics accusing the government of using the intervention for political gain.

Internationally, the intervention strained U.S.-Caribbean relations. The Caribbean nations expressed their disapproval of the intervention, viewing it as a violation of their sovereignty. The diplomatic repercussions were felt for years, as the U.S. faced criticism from many nations for its unilateral actions in Grenada.

In conclusion, the legality of the 1983 U.S. military intervention in Grenada remains a subject of debate. While the U.S. government justified the intervention under the principles of self-defense and collective security, critics questioned the legitimacy of these justifications. The lack of a Security Council resolution further complicated the legal arguments. The intervention's consequences extended beyond legal debates, impacting regional stability, diplomatic relations, and the U.S.'s international reputation.

Reactions from international legal organizations and institutions

The 1983 U.S. military intervention in Grenada raised significant concerns among international legal organizations and institutions. Many of these entities questioned the legality and justification of the intervention, leading to a range of reactions and consequences.

One of the primary organizations to express its concerns was the United Nations (UN). The UN Security Council held an emergency meeting to discuss the situation in Grenada and passed a resolution condemning the U.S. military intervention. The resolution called for a withdrawal of all foreign military forces and a restoration of constitutional order in Grenada. This reaction highlighted the international community's commitment to upholding the principles of sovereignty and non-intervention.

Additionally, the Organization of American States (OAS) also voiced its disapproval of the U.S. intervention. The OAS passed a resolution expressing concern over the violation of Grenada's sovereignty and called for a peaceful resolution to the conflict. This reaction showcased the regional implications of the intervention and the importance of maintaining stability and cooperation among neighboring countries.

The International Court of Justice (ICJ), the principal judicial organ of the UN, received a request from Grenada to issue an advisory opinion on the legality of the U.S. military intervention. Although the ICJ declined to provide an opinion on the matter, the request itself underscored Grenada's determination to challenge the intervention's legality through international legal channels.

Furthermore, various human rights organizations, such as Amnesty International and Human Rights Watch, condemned the intervention due to concerns about potential human rights abuses and violations. These organizations called for an investigation into allegations of excessive use of force, arbitrary detentions, and violations of the rights of civilians caught in the crossfire.

The reactions from these international legal organizations and institutions had a lasting impact on the perception and understanding of the intervention. They contributed to the ongoing debate surrounding the legality and morality of the U.S. military intervention in Grenada. Additionally, these reactions prompted discussions on the role of international law in shaping military interventions and the need for accountability in such operations.

Overall, the reactions from international legal organizations and institutions shed light on the complexities and controversies surrounding the 1983 U.S. military intervention in Grenada. Historians examining the intervention and its consequences will find these reactions to be crucial in understanding the broader international context and the implications for regional stability, diplomatic relations, and the role of intelligence agencies in shaping military interventions.

Lessons learned for future military interventions

The 1983 U.S. military intervention in Grenada marked a significant moment in history, with far-reaching consequences that continue to shape international relations and military strategies today. As historians, it is essential to reflect on the lessons learned from this intervention, in order to improve future military operations and mitigate potential negative outcomes.

One of the key lessons from the intervention in Grenada is the importance of clear objectives and a well-defined exit strategy. The lack of a clear end goal in Grenada led to an extended presence and an uncertain timeline for withdrawal. Future interventions must establish achievable objectives and a concrete plan for disengagement to prevent prolonged military involvement.

Additionally, the political implications of military interventions must be thoroughly considered. In the case of Grenada, the intervention raised questions about sovereignty and the potential for interventionist policies. Historians must analyze the political factors that contributed to the intervention and assess the impact on regional stability and diplomatic relations. Understanding these implications will inform future decision-making processes and ensure a more nuanced approach to military interventions.

The role of intelligence agencies in planning military interventions should also be carefully examined. In the case of Grenada, intelligence failures led to certain miscalculations and limited understanding of the situation on the ground. Historians must explore the shortcomings and successes of intelligence gathering and analysis to enhance the effectiveness of future interventions.

Furthermore, the media coverage of the intervention in Grenada highlights the need for greater transparency and accurate reporting. Historians should analyze the media's role in shaping public opinion and influencing policy decisions. This understanding will help in crafting more responsible and informed media strategies during future military interventions.

Lastly, the humanitarian aspects of military interventions require extensive consideration. Historians must evaluate the impact on civilian populations, ensuring that humanitarian aid and protection are prioritized. Lessons learned from Grenada can be used to develop protocols and guidelines to minimize harm and prioritize the well-being of affected communities.

In conclusion, the 1983 U.S. military intervention in Grenada offers valuable lessons for future military interventions. By considering the political, diplomatic, intelligence, media, and humanitarian aspects, historians can contribute to the development of more effective and responsible military strategies. Learning from the past is crucial in order to avoid repeating mistakes and to ensure that future interventions are conducted with the utmost care and consideration.

Chapter 6: The Media Coverage of the 1983 U.S. Military Intervention in Grenada

Media portrayal of the intervention and its consequences

The media portrayal of the 1983 U.S. military intervention in Grenada played a significant role in shaping public perception and understanding of the event. Journalists faced numerous challenges in reporting on the intervention, including limited access to accurate information, censorship, and the need to balance national security concerns with the public's right to know.

In the immediate aftermath of the intervention, media coverage largely focused on the military aspects of the operation. News outlets highlighted the successful rescue of American students and the overthrow of the Marxist government. These reports presented the intervention as a necessary response to protect American lives and promote democracy in the region. The portrayal of the intervention as a swift and decisive military victory bolstered public support for the operation.

However, as more information became available, media coverage began to shift. Journalists began to question the legality and justification of the intervention, particularly in light of international law. Reports highlighted the lack of a clear legal mandate from the United Nations and raised concerns about the potential precedent set by unilateral military interventions. This critical analysis prompted a more nuanced understanding of the intervention and its consequences.

The media also played a crucial role in shedding light on the humanitarian aspects of the intervention. Journalists reported on the conditions in Grenada before and after the intervention, documenting human rights abuses and the need for humanitarian assistance. These reports highlighted the complexities of the situation and challenged the narrative of a purely benevolent military intervention.

The media coverage of the intervention had significant political implications. Criticism of the intervention grew, both domestically and internationally, leading to increased scrutiny of U.S. foreign policy. The media's role in shaping public opinion and holding governments accountable became evident during this period.

Furthermore, the media coverage of the intervention had a lasting impact on U.S.-Caribbean relations. The intervention strained diplomatic ties between the United States and other Caribbean nations, who viewed the operation as an infringement on their sovereignty. The media portrayal of the intervention contributed to a sense of mistrust and resentment towards the United States, which had far-reaching consequences for regional stability.

In conclusion, the media portrayal of the 1983 U.S. military intervention in Grenada played a crucial role in shaping public perception and understanding of the event. Journalists faced numerous challenges in reporting on the intervention, but their coverage ultimately shed light on the complexities and consequences of the operation. The media's critical analysis of the intervention's legality, its humanitarian aspects, and its political and diplomatic implications provided a more nuanced understanding of the intervention and its impact on U.S.-Caribbean relations.

Influence on public opinion in the United States and globally

The 1983 U.S. military intervention in Grenada was not only a significant event in the history of the Caribbean, but it also had a profound impact on public opinion both in the United States and globally. Understanding the influence on public opinion is crucial to comprehending the broader implications and consequences of this military intervention.

In the United States, public opinion played a pivotal role in shaping the government's response to the crisis in Grenada. The Reagan administration, facing a multitude of challenges both domestically and internationally, sought to portray the intervention as necessary to protect American citizens and to prevent the spread of communism in the region. Through skillful manipulation of media coverage and strategic messaging, the administration was able to sway public opinion in favor of the intervention. The media coverage predominantly portrayed the intervention as a necessary and justifiable action, highlighting the rescue of American medical students and the restoration of stability in Grenada.

Globally, the intervention in Grenada had mixed reactions. Some countries, particularly those aligned with the United States, supported the intervention and echoed the administration's claims of protecting democracy and regional stability. However, other nations, particularly those critical of American foreign policy, viewed the intervention as an infringement on Grenada's sovereignty and a violation of international law. This diversity of opinion reflected the complex geopolitical landscape of the time and highlighted the differing perspectives on the role of interventionism in international affairs.

The influence on public opinion in relation to the 1983 U.S. military intervention in Grenada had far-reaching consequences. Domestically, it bolstered the Reagan administration's credibility and strengthened its position both within the United States and on the global stage. However, it also raised important questions about the role of intelligence agencies in shaping public opinion and the potential for manipulation in the media.

Historians studying this period must recognize the interplay between public opinion, media coverage, and political decision-making. By examining the influence on public opinion, historians can gain a deeper understanding of the motivations behind the intervention, its impact on regional stability, and its long-term repercussions on U.S.-Caribbean relations. Additionally, analyzing the global reaction to the intervention provides insights into the complex dynamics of international relations and the divergent perspectives on the use of military force.

Overall, the influence on public opinion surrounding the 1983 U.S. military intervention in Grenada serves as a reminder of the power of media, strategic messaging, and intelligence agencies in shaping public perception and influencing political decision-making. By delving into this topic, historians can shed light on the multifaceted nature of this intervention and its lasting impact on both domestic and international affairs.

Analysis of media bias and representation of the events

In the subchapter titled "Analysis of Media Bias and Representation of the Events," we delve into the critical examination of how the media covered the 1983 U.S. military intervention in Grenada. This analysis is crucial for historians studying various aspects of this intervention and its consequences, as it sheds light on the role of media in shaping public perception and the implications it had on the events and aftermath.

The media coverage of the 1983 U.S. military intervention in Grenada was marked by significant bias and varying degrees of representation. Historians interested in understanding the political implications and diplomatic repercussions of this intervention must carefully scrutinize the media's portrayal of the events.

Firstly, it is essential to examine the biases that permeated media coverage. Some media outlets aligned themselves with the U.S.

government's narrative, framing the intervention as a necessary step to protect American lives and restore stability in the region. Others, however, criticized the intervention as an infringement on Grenada's sovereignty and a violation of international law. Historians must analyze how these biases influenced public opinion and the subsequent political discourse surrounding the intervention.

Moreover, the representation of events in the media played a crucial role in shaping the public's perception of the intervention. The media's focus on specific aspects, such as the military strategies employed, the humanitarian aspects, or the role of intelligence agencies, influenced the public's understanding of the intervention's motives and consequences. Historians must evaluate the accuracy and comprehensiveness of media representation to gain a holistic view of the events.

Additionally, analyzing media bias and representation offers insights into the impact of the intervention on regional stability and U.S.-Caribbean relations. By examining how the media covered these aspects, historians can gauge the public's perception of the intervention's aftermath and its implications for regional dynamics. This analysis also provides valuable information on the role of international law and the diplomatic repercussions of the intervention, both of which are crucial in understanding the broader implications of this historical event.

In conclusion, the analysis of media bias and representation of the events surrounding the 1983 U.S. military intervention in Grenada is a vital component for historians studying various aspects of this intervention and its consequences. By examining the biases and representations in media coverage, historians can gain valuable insights into the political, diplomatic, and regional implications of the intervention, as well as its impact on U.S.-Caribbean relations and international law. This analysis serves as an essential tool for understanding how the media shapes public perception and contributes to the historical narrative surrounding significant events.

Chapter 7: The Military Strategies Employed During the 1983 U.S. Military Intervention in Grenada

Overview of the military operation and objectives

The 1983 U.S. military intervention in Grenada was a significant event in history that had far-reaching consequences, not only for the small Caribbean island but also for regional stability and international relations. This subchapter provides a comprehensive overview of the military operation and its objectives, shedding light on the role of intelligence agencies in the planning process.

The military operation, codenamed Operation Urgent Fury, was launched on October 25, 1983, by the United States following a coup d'état in Grenada. The objectives of the intervention were multi-faceted and included the restoration of order and democracy, the protection of American citizens on the island, and the prevention of the establishment of a Soviet-backed government that could potentially threaten U.S. interests in the region.

The operation involved a joint military force comprising elements from the U.S. Army, Navy, and Marines, as well as special operations forces. The military strategies employed during the intervention were a combination of aerial and amphibious assaults, with an emphasis on swift and decisive action to achieve the stated objectives.

The humanitarian aspects of the intervention cannot be overlooked. The U.S. forces prioritized the safety and well-being of the Grenadian population, providing medical assistance, food, and water to those in need. Additionally, efforts were made to minimize civilian casualties and collateral damage throughout the operation.

The media coverage of the intervention played a significant role in shaping public opinion. Journalists faced numerous challenges in accessing accurate information due to the classified nature of the operation. The limited media coverage led to speculation and misinformation, further fueling debates surrounding the legitimacy and necessity of the intervention.

From a diplomatic perspective, the intervention had wide-ranging repercussions. The U.S.-Caribbean relations were strained due to the unilateral nature of the intervention, with some regional governments expressing their disapproval. The impact on international law and sovereignty was also a subject of debate, as the intervention was carried out without explicit approval from the United Nations.

In conclusion, the 1983 U.S. military intervention in Grenada was a complex operation with multiple objectives and consequences. Understanding the military strategies employed, the humanitarian aspects, and the diplomatic repercussions is crucial for historians and those interested in the aftermath of the intervention. Furthermore, exploring the role of intelligence agencies in planning the operation sheds light on the intricate web of intelligence gathering and decision-making that shaped this historical event. The impact of the intervention on regional stability and U.S.-Caribbean relations cannot be underestimated, making it a significant chapter in modern history.

Assessment of the effectiveness of military tactics and strategies

The 1983 U.S. military intervention in Grenada was a highly controversial event that had far-reaching consequences. In order to understand the full implications of this intervention, it is essential to assess the effectiveness of the military tactics and strategies employed during this operation.

The U.S. military intervention in Grenada was primarily aimed at removing the Marxist-Leninist government that had come to power through a coup d'état. The operation involved a combination of air and ground forces, with the objective of securing the safety of American citizens on the island and restoring democratic governance. The military tactics employed during this intervention consisted of a rapid and overwhelming show of force, with a focus on achieving key objectives within a short timeframe.

From a strategic standpoint, the U.S. military intervention in Grenada can be considered a success. The operation achieved its primary objectives, including the removal of the revolutionary government and the restoration of political stability. The swift and decisive nature of the intervention sent a strong message to other potential adversaries and demonstrated the U.S. commitment to upholding democratic values.

However, the military tactics employed during the intervention also raised concerns and generated criticism. The speed and scale of the operation led to a lack of coordination between different military units, resulting in some instances of friendly fire and civilian casualties. Additionally, the limited intelligence available prior to the intervention resulted in some misjudgments and miscalculations, which could have been avoided with better planning and information gathering.

In assessing the effectiveness of military tactics and strategies, it is important to consider the broader consequences of the intervention. The aftermath of the 1983 U.S. military intervention in Grenada saw a period of political instability and social unrest. The intervention also had implications for regional stability, with neighboring countries concerned about the potential for further military interventions in the Caribbean.

Furthermore, the diplomatic repercussions of the intervention were significant. The United Nations General Assembly condemned the intervention as a violation of international law, while some countries, particularly in the Non-Aligned Movement, criticized the U.S. for its unilateral action. The media coverage of the intervention also played a crucial role in shaping public opinion and influencing the international discourse surrounding the event.

In conclusion, the assessment of the effectiveness of military tactics and strategies employed during the 1983 U.S. military intervention in Grenada is a complex task. While the operation achieved its primary objectives, there were also shortcomings and unintended consequences. Understanding the impact of this intervention requires a comprehensive analysis of its political, diplomatic, and humanitarian aspects, as well as the role played by intelligence agencies in the planning process. By examining these different dimensions, historians can gain valuable insights into the far-reaching implications of this pivotal event in U.S.-Caribbean relations.

Lessons learned for future military operations

The 1983 U.S. military intervention in Grenada was a significant event in history that had far-reaching consequences. As historians examine this event and its aftermath, there are several valuable lessons that can be learned for future military operations.

First and foremost, the importance of accurate and timely intelligence cannot be overstated. The role of intelligence agencies in planning the intervention was crucial, but there were also instances where intelligence failures occurred. It is essential for future military operations to prioritize intelligence gathering and ensure that it is reliable and up-to-date. This will enable decision-makers to make informed choices and avoid costly mistakes.

Another lesson learned is the significance of understanding the political implications of military interventions. The aftermath of the 1983 intervention in Grenada highlighted the importance of considering the long-term political consequences of such actions. Future military operations should take into account the potential impact on local politics and work towards fostering stability and sustainable governance in the region.

Additionally, the media coverage of the intervention played a significant role in shaping public perception and international opinion. The lessons learned from this aspect of the intervention include the need for effective communication strategies and transparency. Future military operations should prioritize clear and accurate communication to ensure public understanding and support.

The humanitarian aspects of the intervention also provide valuable lessons. It is crucial for military operations to consider and prioritize the well-being and safety of civilians in conflict zones. Humanitarian aid and assistance should be coordinated and delivered effectively to mitigate the impact on civilian populations.

Furthermore, the diplomatic repercussions of the intervention highlight the importance of international collaboration and adherence to international law. Future military operations should be conducted in accordance with international legal frameworks and in coordination with relevant international bodies. This will help mitigate potential diplomatic tensions and maintain positive relations with other nations.

Lastly, the impact of the intervention on U.S.-Caribbean relations underscores the need for a nuanced approach to regional stability. Military interventions should be carefully considered within the broader context of regional dynamics and should strive to foster long-term stability and cooperation.

In conclusion, the lessons learned from the 1983 U.S. military intervention in Grenada provide valuable insights for future military operations. These include the importance of accurate intelligence, understanding political implications, effective communication, prioritizing humanitarian aspects, adhering to international law, and considering regional dynamics. By applying these lessons, future military operations can strive for better outcomes and minimize negative consequences.

Chapter 8: The Humanitarian Aspects of the 1983 U.S. Military Intervention in Grenada

Provision of aid and assistance to the Grenadian population

The 1983 U.S. military intervention in Grenada had far-reaching consequences that extended beyond the realm of politics and military strategy. One crucial aspect that cannot be overlooked is the provision of aid and assistance to the Grenadian population during and after the intervention.

During the military operation, it became evident that the Grenadian people were in dire need of immediate humanitarian aid. The intervention disrupted essential services such as healthcare, electricity, and water supply, leaving the population in a vulnerable state. The U.S. military, in collaboration with international organizations and neighboring Caribbean nations, swiftly mobilized to address these urgent needs.

Medical teams were deployed to provide emergency healthcare services to the Grenadian population. Field hospitals were set up to treat the wounded and provide much-needed medical supplies. Additionally, efforts were made to restore the healthcare infrastructure, including the reopening of hospitals and clinics.

The provision of food and water was another critical aspect of the humanitarian response. The intervention disrupted the food supply chain, leading to shortages and hunger among the population. The U.S. military, along with international aid organizations, initiated airlifts of food and water to alleviate the immediate crisis. Distribution centers were established to ensure equitable access to these essential supplies.

Furthermore, efforts were made to restore basic services such as electricity and water supply. The U.S. military, in coordination with local authorities and international partners, worked to repair damaged infrastructure and restore these vital services to the Grenadian people.

In the aftermath of the intervention, the provision of aid and assistance continued. Reconstruction projects were implemented to rebuild schools, hospitals, and other critical infrastructure. The U.S. government, along with international donors, provided financial support for these initiatives to facilitate the recovery process.

The provision of aid and assistance to the Grenadian population not only addressed immediate humanitarian needs but also played a crucial role in stabilizing the region. By demonstrating a commitment to the well-being of the Grenadian people, the U.S. military intervention aimed to win the hearts and minds of the local population and prevent potential backlash or resistance.

In conclusion, the provision of aid and assistance to the Grenadian population was a vital component of the 1983 U.S. military intervention in Grenada. By addressing immediate humanitarian needs and supporting long-term recovery efforts, the intervention aimed to stabilize the region and foster positive U.S.-Caribbean relations. This aspect of the intervention is crucial to understanding the full impact of the operation and its consequences on both the Grenadian population and broader international relations.

Impact on human rights and humanitarian efforts in Grenada

Title: Impact on Human Rights and Humanitarian Efforts in Grenada

The 1983 U.S. military intervention in Grenada had significant consequences on various aspects of the nation's socio-political landscape, particularly concerning human rights and humanitarian efforts. This subchapter delves into the far-reaching implications of the intervention, shedding light on the challenges faced by Grenada in the aftermath of the military operation.

One of the primary concerns following the intervention was the impact on human rights. Historically, Grenada had been governed by Marxist-Leninist principles under the People's Revolutionary Government (PRG). While the PRG was widely criticized for its human rights abuses, the U.S. military intervention raised questions about the violation of Grenadian sovereignty and the potential disregard for international law.

The humanitarian aspects of the intervention were also significant. The sudden military operation disrupted essential services, including healthcare and education, further exacerbating the already fragile socio-economic conditions in Grenada. Additionally, the intervention resulted in civilian casualties, raising concerns about the protection of innocent lives and the adherence to humanitarian principles.

The aftermath of the intervention witnessed efforts to restore democratic governance and rebuild the nation's institutions. However, the process was not without challenges. The U.S.-backed transition faced criticism for not adequately involving local stakeholders and for prioritizing American interests over Grenadian aspirations. This raised questions about the true intentions and long-term implications of the intervention on the political stability of the region.

Furthermore, the diplomatic repercussions of the intervention were felt both regionally and internationally. The intervention strained relations between the United States and the Caribbean nations, as some viewed it as an infringement on the principle of non-intervention in the internal affairs of sovereign states. The event also highlighted the role of intelligence agencies in planning military operations, raising concerns about the transparency and accountability of such operations.

In examining the impact on U.S.-Caribbean relations, it becomes apparent that the intervention left a lasting mark. Despite subsequent efforts to repair relations, the intervention created a sense of mistrust and unease, shaping the dynamics between the United States and the Caribbean for years to come.

To fully comprehend the implications of the 1983 U.S. military intervention in Grenada, it is crucial to examine its impact on human rights and humanitarian efforts. This subchapter provides a comprehensive analysis of the consequences faced by Grenada, shedding light on the challenges encountered in the aftermath of the intervention and the lasting effects on both the nation and the wider Caribbean region.

Evaluation of the humanitarian response and its effectiveness

The 1983 U.S. military intervention in Grenada was a complex operation that had far-reaching consequences, both regionally and internationally. Among the various aspects of this intervention, the humanitarian response played a crucial role in mitigating the impact of the conflict on the local population. This subchapter aims to evaluate the effectiveness of the humanitarian response and shed light on its implications for historians and individuals interested in the aftermath of the intervention.

During the intervention, humanitarian aid was provided to the people of Grenada by both the United States and other countries in the region. This aid included medical assistance, food supplies, and infrastructure restoration efforts. The primary objective was to alleviate the suffering caused by the conflict and ensure the well-being of the affected population.

In evaluating the effectiveness of the humanitarian response, it is crucial to consider the immediate and long-term outcomes. In the immediate aftermath of the intervention, the provision of aid had a significant impact on saving lives and meeting the basic needs of the population. Medical teams from various countries were able to provide emergency care and treat the wounded. Additionally, food and water supplies were distributed to alleviate hunger and ensure survival.

However, the effectiveness of the humanitarian response was not without challenges. The rapid deployment of aid teams and resources faced logistical obstacles due to the ongoing military operations. Furthermore, the coordination between different organizations and agencies involved in the response efforts was not always seamless, leading to delays and duplication of efforts.

In the long term, the humanitarian response helped in the reconstruction and development of Grenada. Efforts were made to rebuild infrastructure, restore educational institutions, and create sustainable livelihoods for the affected population. These initiatives aimed to ensure that Grenada could recover from the conflict and achieve stability.

The evaluation of the humanitarian response also raises important questions about the role of international law and the diplomatic repercussions of the intervention. The intervention itself sparked debates about the legality of the military action and the extent to which it was justified under international law. Additionally, the response efforts highlighted the importance of international cooperation and coordination in addressing humanitarian crises.

Overall, the evaluation of the humanitarian response and its effectiveness provides valuable insights into the consequences of the 1983 U.S. military intervention in Grenada. It highlights the importance of addressing the immediate needs of the affected population and the challenges involved in coordinating international aid efforts during times of conflict. Moreover, it underscores the long-term implications of such interventions on the socio-economic development and political stability of the region.

Chapter 9: The Diplomatic Repercussions of the 1983 U.S. Military Intervention in Grenada

Responses from other nations and international organizations

The 1983 U.S. military intervention in Grenada sent shockwaves throughout the international community. Numerous nations and international organizations responded to this unprecedented event, each with their own perspectives and concerns. This subchapter explores the responses from other nations and international organizations, shedding light on the global implications of this military intervention.

Immediately following the intervention, neighboring Caribbean nations expressed mixed reactions. Some countries, such as Jamaica, Barbados, and Trinidad and Tobago, expressed their support for the U.S. action, citing concerns about the stability of the region and the threat posed by the Marxist-Leninist government in Grenada. However, others, including Cuba and Nicaragua, strongly condemned the intervention as a violation of international law and an imperialistic act by the United States.

Beyond the Caribbean, the response was also varied. The United Kingdom, as Grenada's former colonial power, expressed initial concerns over the lack of consultation but ultimately supported the intervention. Many Western European nations, such as France and Germany, expressed reservations about the unilateral nature of the U.S. action but refrained from outright condemnation. The Soviet Union and its allies, on the other hand, vehemently condemned the intervention and accused the United States of aggression.

International organizations, such as the United Nations (UN) and the Organization of American States (OAS), also responded to the intervention. The UN General Assembly passed a resolution condemning the U.S. military action, while the Security Council failed to reach a consensus due to the veto power of the United States. The OAS, despite divisions among its member states, ultimately passed a resolution calling for the withdrawal of foreign troops from Grenada and the restoration of democratic governance.

These responses from other nations and international organizations highlighted the complex and divisive nature of the 1983 U.S. military intervention in Grenada. They also underscored the divergent interpretations of international law and the principles of sovereignty and non-intervention. The aftermath of the intervention saw a reevaluation of international norms and a renewed focus on the role of regional stability and diplomatic relations.

As historians delve into this chapter, they will gain a deeper understanding of the global repercussions of the 1983 U.S. military intervention in Grenada. By examining the responses from other nations and international organizations, they can analyze the political, diplomatic, and legal implications of this controversial event. This subchapter offers valuable insights into the multifaceted nature of the intervention and its lasting impact on U.S.-Caribbean relations, regional stability, and international law.

Diplomatic negotiations and efforts to resolve conflicts

The subchapter on diplomatic negotiations and efforts to resolve conflicts in the book "Secret Operations: The Role of Intelligence Agencies in Planning the 1983 U.S. Military Intervention in Grenada and Its Consequences" sheds light on the various diplomatic initiatives taken before and during the U.S. military intervention in Grenada. This section provides historians with a comprehensive analysis of the diplomatic landscape during that crucial period in history.

The chapter begins by examining the attempts made by regional and international actors to resolve the conflicts in Grenada through peaceful means. It delves into the diplomatic efforts of the Caribbean Community (CARICOM), the Organization of Eastern Caribbean States (OECS), and the United Nations (UN) to mediate between the warring factions in Grenada. These diplomatic negotiations, although well-intentioned, ultimately failed to achieve a peaceful resolution to the crisis.

The subchapter then explores the role of the United States in the diplomatic arena. It discusses the behind-the-scenes negotiations conducted by U.S. diplomats with various regional and international actors, including the Grenadian government, other Caribbean nations, and major global powers. These negotiations aimed to find a diplomatic solution and avoid military intervention. However, as the book reveals, the U.S. government's determination to remove the communist regime in Grenada and perceived threats to American citizens eventually led to the decision to intervene militarily.

Furthermore, the chapter analyzes the diplomatic repercussions of the U.S. military intervention in Grenada. It examines the reactions of regional and international actors, the United Nations, and the Organization of American States (OAS) to the intervention. It explores the criticisms and support received by the United States, as well as the long-term impact on U.S.-Caribbean relations.

The subchapter also addresses the role of intelligence agencies in shaping diplomatic negotiations and efforts to resolve conflicts. It explores how intelligence reports and analysis influenced decision-making processes and informed diplomatic initiatives. It sheds light on the intelligence community's assessments of the situation in Grenada and their impact on the diplomatic channels.

Overall, this subchapter provides historians with a comprehensive understanding of the diplomatic dynamics surrounding the 1983 U.S. military intervention in Grenada. It explores the various attempts made to resolve the conflict peacefully, the role of the United States in diplomatic negotiations, the diplomatic repercussions of the intervention, and the influence of intelligence agencies on diplomatic efforts. By examining these aspects, historians can gain valuable insights into the complexities of diplomatic decision-making during this critical period in history.

Long-term effects on diplomatic relations and international cooperation

The 1983 U.S. military intervention in Grenada marked a significant turning point in diplomatic relations and international cooperation. The aftermath of the intervention had far-reaching consequences that continue to shape the political landscape and regional stability of the Caribbean. This subchapter delves into the long-term effects of the intervention on various aspects, including diplomatic repercussions, international law, and intelligence agency involvement.

One of the most evident long-term effects of the intervention was the strain it placed on diplomatic relations. The United States' unilateral decision to invade Grenada without obtaining prior approval from the United Nations or regional organizations like the Organization of American States (OAS) raised concerns about respect for international norms and sovereignty. This led to a rupture in U.S.-Caribbean relations, as many countries in the region viewed the intervention as an infringement on their autonomy and a violation of the principles of non-interference.

Furthermore, the intervention highlighted the complex relationship between international law and military interventions. The lack of a clear legal mandate for the invasion raised questions about the role of international law in regulating such actions. This event prompted a reevaluation of the legal framework governing military interventions and sparked discussions on the need for stricter guidelines to prevent future violations of sovereignty.

The media coverage of the intervention also played a significant role in shaping diplomatic relations. The portrayal of the U.S. military intervention in Grenada varied across different media outlets, with some highlighting the perceived humanitarian aspects of the intervention while others criticized it for its aggressive and unilateral nature. The media coverage influenced public opinion, both domestically and internationally, and contributed to the perception of the United States as an imperial power.

Moreover, the intervention had broader implications for regional stability. The military strategies employed during the intervention, such as the rapid deployment of troops and the use of overwhelming force, sent a powerful message to other countries in the region. This display of military might had a deterrent effect on potential adversaries, but it also heightened tensions and mistrust among neighboring nations.

Lastly, the role of intelligence agencies in planning the intervention cannot be overlooked. The covert operations and intelligence gathering conducted by these agencies played a crucial role in shaping the decision-making process. The intervention highlighted the significant influence intelligence agencies have on foreign policy and raised questions about the transparency and accountability of their actions.

In conclusion, the long-term effects of the 1983 U.S. military intervention in Grenada on diplomatic relations and international cooperation were profound. The intervention strained diplomatic ties, sparked discussions on international law, influenced media coverage, impacted regional stability, and shed light on the role of intelligence agencies. Understanding these long-term effects is crucial for historians and researchers studying this pivotal event in history.

Chapter 10: The Role of Intelligence Agencies in Planning the 1983 U.S. Military Intervention in Grenada

Overview of the intelligence gathering process and agencies involved

In order to fully understand the planning and execution of the 1983 U.S. military intervention in Grenada, it is essential to examine the intelligence gathering process and the various agencies involved. Intelligence plays a crucial role in shaping military operations, informing decision-makers, and ensuring the success of any military intervention. This subchapter will provide an overview of the intelligence gathering process and highlight the key agencies involved in planning the 1983 U.S. military intervention in Grenada.

The intelligence gathering process encompasses a wide range of activities, including collection, analysis, and dissemination of information. Intelligence agencies are responsible for gathering data through various sources, such as human intelligence (HUMINT), signals intelligence (SIGINT), imagery intelligence (IMINT), and open-source intelligence (OSINT). These agencies employ highly trained personnel who specialize in specific intelligence disciplines to ensure comprehensive coverage.

In the case of the 1983 U.S. military intervention in Grenada, several intelligence agencies played crucial roles. The Central Intelligence Agency (CIA) was at the forefront of intelligence gathering efforts, utilizing its vast network of agents and informants to provide valuable insights into Grenada's political, military, and social landscape. The Defense Intelligence Agency (DIA) also contributed significantly by analyzing military capabilities and providing threat assessments.

Furthermore, the National Security Agency (NSA) played a pivotal role in intercepting and decoding communications, providing critical SIGINT to support the planning and execution of the intervention. The National Reconnaissance Office (NRO) provided IMINT through satellite reconnaissance, offering valuable imagery of Grenada's infrastructure, military installations, and potential targets.

Cooperation and coordination among these agencies were paramount to ensure the availability and accuracy of intelligence. Regular intelligence briefings were held, where representatives from different agencies shared their findings and assessments. These briefings allowed decision-makers to have a comprehensive understanding of the situation in Grenada and tailor their military strategies accordingly.

The intelligence gathering process for the 1983 U.S. military intervention in Grenada was not without challenges. Limited resources, language barriers, and the complex nature of intelligence collection in a hostile environment posed significant obstacles. However, the agencies involved employed innovative techniques and leveraged their expertise to overcome these challenges.

In conclusion, the intelligence gathering process and the involvement of various agencies were critical in planning the 1983 U.S. military intervention in Grenada. The CIA, DIA, NSA, and NRO played instrumental roles in collecting, analyzing, and disseminating intelligence. Their efforts ensured that decision-makers had access to accurate and timely information, which ultimately influenced the success of the intervention. Understanding the intelligence gathering process and the agencies involved provides a comprehensive perspective on the planning and execution of the 1983 U.S. military intervention in Grenada, making it an essential aspect for historians and those interested in the niche topics related to this historical event.

Analysis of intelligence assessments and their influence on decision-making

Intelligence assessments play a crucial role in shaping decision-making processes, especially in matters of national security and military interventions. This subchapter delves into the analysis of intelligence assessments and their influence on the planning and execution of the 1983 U.S. military intervention in Grenada, shedding light on the complexities of intelligence gathering and its implications on historical events.

Historians studying the 1983 U.S. military intervention in Grenada will find this analysis particularly valuable as it dissects the role of intelligence agencies in the planning stages of the operation. The subchapter explores the intelligence community's efforts to gather information, assess potential threats, and provide policymakers with accurate and timely intelligence assessments. It examines the various intelligence sources, methodologies, and techniques employed to gather information on Grenada, including human intelligence, signals intelligence, and imagery intelligence.

Furthermore, this analysis critically evaluates the accuracy and reliability of the intelligence assessments used to justify the military intervention. Historians will gain insights into the limitations, biases, and gaps in the intelligence gathered, as well as the challenges faced by intelligence analysts during this period.

The subchapter also explores how intelligence assessments influenced decision-making at the highest levels of government. It examines the process by which intelligence reports were analyzed, synthesized, and presented to policymakers, highlighting the extent to which these assessments shaped the narrative surrounding the need for military intervention in Grenada. By examining the interaction between intelligence agencies and decision-makers, historians can gain a deeper understanding of the factors that influenced the ultimate decision to intervene militarily.

Moreover, this analysis sheds light on the consequences of the intelligence assessments on the aftermath of the military intervention. It explores how the accuracy or inaccuracy of the intelligence influenced the outcomes, both intended and unintended, of the operation. Historians interested in the political implications, regional stability, and diplomatic repercussions of the intervention will find this analysis particularly relevant.

Overall, this subchapter serves as a comprehensive examination of the analysis of intelligence assessments and their influence on decision-making in the context of the 1983 U.S. military intervention in Grenada. It offers historians a nuanced understanding of the role played by intelligence agencies in shaping historical events and their impact on various aspects of the intervention, from regional stability to U.S.-Caribbean relations.

Evaluation of the role and effectiveness of intelligence agencies in the intervention

Intelligence agencies play a crucial role in the planning and execution of military interventions, and the 1983 U.S. military intervention in Grenada was no exception. This subchapter aims to evaluate the role and effectiveness of intelligence agencies in this particular operation, shedding light on their contributions, successes, and failures.

The intelligence agencies involved in the planning of the Grenada intervention, primarily the Central Intelligence Agency (CIA) and the Defense Intelligence Agency (DIA), were responsible for gathering and analyzing information crucial for decision-making. Their primary objective was to provide accurate and timely intelligence to policymakers, military commanders, and other relevant stakeholders.

One of the main successes of intelligence agencies in this intervention was their ability to identify and assess the threat posed by the Marxist government of Grenada, led by Prime Minister Maurice Bishop. Through covert operations and surveillance, they were able to gather valuable information on the military capabilities, intentions, and alliances of the Grenadian government. This intelligence was instrumental in justifying the intervention and ensuring its success.

However, intelligence agencies also faced challenges and shortcomings in their role. One notable failure was their inability to accurately predict the timing and extent of the internal power struggle within the Grenadian government, which ultimately led to the execution of Prime Minister Bishop and the subsequent military coup. This lack of foresight compromised the overall intelligence picture and had implications for the intervention's objectives.

Additionally, the intelligence community's handling of the aftermath of the intervention came under scrutiny. There were concerns about the accuracy and reliability of intelligence reports on the ground situation post-intervention. This led to questions about the effectiveness of intelligence agencies in providing reliable information during the critical phase of stabilization and nation-building.

In conclusion, the role of intelligence agencies in planning the 1983 U.S. military intervention in Grenada was significant. They provided critical intelligence that shaped policy decisions and ensured the success of the intervention. However, there were also limitations and failures that impacted the overall effectiveness of intelligence efforts. Historians studying this intervention should consider the complex and multifaceted role of intelligence agencies, acknowledging both their contributions and areas for improvement. Understanding the successes and failures in intelligence operations during this intervention can provide valuable insights into the broader context of intelligence planning and execution in military interventions.

Chapter 11: The Impact of the 1983 U.S. Military Intervention in Grenada on U.S.-Caribbean Relations

Changes in U.S. foreign policy towards the Caribbean region

Throughout history, the United States has experienced significant shifts in its foreign policy towards the Caribbean region. These changes have had far-reaching implications, particularly in the aftermath of the 1983 U.S. military intervention in Grenada. Understanding these shifts is crucial for historians and those interested in various aspects of this intervention, including its political implications, impact on regional stability, role of international law, media coverage, military strategies employed, humanitarian aspects, diplomatic repercussions, and the role of intelligence agencies.

The 1983 U.S. military intervention in Grenada marked a turning point in U.S. foreign policy towards the Caribbean region. Prior to this intervention, the U.S. had largely followed a policy of non-intervention and non-interference in the affairs of Caribbean nations. However, the rise of the New Jewel Movement in Grenada, with its Marxist-Leninist ideology and close ties to Cuba and the Soviet Union, raised concerns about the spread of communism in the region.

As a result, the U.S. shifted its foreign policy towards a more interventionist approach. The intervention in Grenada was justified on the grounds of protecting American citizens, restoring democracy, and preventing the establishment of a Soviet-Cuban military base. This marked a departure from the non-interventionist stance and signaled a willingness to act militarily to safeguard American interests in the region.

The aftermath of the intervention had significant political implications. The U.S.-backed installation of a new government in Grenada sparked debates about the legitimacy of foreign intervention and the violation of national sovereignty. These discussions continue to shape the discourse on international relations and the role of powerful nations in smaller, developing countries.

Furthermore, the intervention had a profound impact on regional stability. While it achieved its immediate goals of removing the Marxist government and preventing the establishment of a Soviet-Cuban military base, it also disrupted the delicate balance of power in the Caribbean. The intervention highlighted the vulnerability of smaller nations in the face of larger, more powerful actors and raised concerns about the potential for future interventions in the region.

The role of international law in the intervention and its aftermath also warrants examination. Critics argued that the U.S. intervention violated principles of sovereignty and non-interference enshrined in international law. This raises important questions about the efficacy and enforcement of international legal norms in the face of powerful actors.

Media coverage of the intervention played a crucial role in shaping public perception and understanding of the events in Grenada. The media's portrayal of the intervention and its aftermath influenced public opinion, both domestically and internationally. This highlights the power of media narratives in shaping historical memory and the importance of critically analyzing media coverage.

The military strategies employed during the intervention also deserve scrutiny. The U.S. military utilized a combination of air and ground operations to swiftly remove the Marxist government. The success of these strategies raises questions about the efficacy and ethics of military intervention, particularly in smaller, less developed countries.

In addition to its military and political dimensions, the humanitarian aspects of the intervention cannot be overlooked. The intervention resulted in civilian casualties and raised questions about the extent to which humanitarian concerns should factor into foreign policy decisions.

Diplomatically, the intervention had repercussions for U.S.-Caribbean relations. While some Caribbean nations expressed support for the intervention, others condemned it as a violation of sovereignty. This event strained relations between the U.S. and certain Caribbean nations, underscoring the complexities of maintaining diplomatic ties in the wake of military interventions.

Lastly, the role of intelligence agencies in planning the intervention is a crucial aspect to consider. The extent to which intelligence agencies influenced the decision-making process and the accuracy of the information provided raise important questions about the role of intelligence in shaping foreign policy.

In conclusion, the changes in U.S. foreign policy towards the Caribbean region, particularly in the aftermath of the 1983 military intervention in Grenada, have had wide-ranging implications. These changes have impacted political dynamics, regional stability, international law, media coverage, military strategies, humanitarian aspects, diplomatic relations, and the role of intelligence agencies. Understanding these changes is essential for historians and those interested in various niches surrounding this intervention. By analyzing and critically examining these shifts, we can gain valuable insights into the complexities of U.S.-Caribbean relations and the broader implications of foreign policy decisions.

Assessment of the impact on bilateral relations with Caribbean nations

The 1983 U.S. military intervention in Grenada had a significant impact on bilateral relations with Caribbean nations. This subchapter aims to analyze and evaluate the consequences of the intervention in terms of how it affected the relationships between the United States and its Caribbean neighbors.

The military intervention in Grenada created a sense of unease among Caribbean nations, particularly those with left-leaning governments or sympathies. The United States' decision to militarily intervene in the internal affairs of a sovereign nation raised concerns about the potential infringement of Caribbean nations' autonomy and independence. Countries such as Jamaica, Barbados, and Trinidad and Tobago, which had established diplomatic ties with Grenada, expressed their disapproval of the intervention and condemned the U.S.'s actions.

Moreover, the intervention in Grenada brought to the forefront the issue of regional stability. Caribbean nations were apprehensive about the potential for further military interventions in the region, which could disrupt the delicate balance of power and jeopardize their own security. The U.S.'s unilateral decision to intervene without seeking regional consensus undermined trust and cooperation among Caribbean nations, leading to a strain in bilateral relations.

The aftermath of the intervention also had political implications for Caribbean nations. The United States' support for the establishment of a democratic government in Grenada was seen by some as an attempt to impose its own political ideology on the region. This perception created divisions among Caribbean nations, with some embracing the U.S.'s intervention as a necessary step towards democracy, while others viewed it as an infringement on Grenada's sovereignty.

Furthermore, the diplomatic repercussions of the intervention were significant. Caribbean nations sought to assert their independence and sovereignty by strengthening regional institutions such as the Caribbean

Community (CARICOM) to counterbalance U.S. influence. This led to a reevaluation of their relationships with the United States, with some nations adopting a more cautious approach towards U.S. initiatives and policies.

In conclusion, the 1983 U.S. military intervention in Grenada had a profound impact on bilateral relations with Caribbean nations. It strained ties, raised concerns about regional stability, and prompted Caribbean nations to assert their autonomy and independence. The repercussions of the intervention continue to shape U.S.-Caribbean relations, highlighting the complex dynamics between global powers and smaller nations in the pursuit of their respective interests.

Long-term implications for U.S.-Caribbean cooperation and engagement

The 1983 U.S. military intervention in Grenada had profound long-term implications for U.S.-Caribbean cooperation and engagement. The aftermath of the intervention highlighted the complex dynamics between the United States and the Caribbean nations, shaping regional stability and diplomatic relations for years to come.

One of the key long-term implications was the erosion of trust between the United States and the Caribbean countries. The intervention was widely viewed as a violation of Grenada's sovereignty and sparked outrage among many Caribbean nations. This led to strained diplomatic relationships and a sense of resentment towards U.S. foreign policy in the region. The United States had to work hard to rebuild trust and restore its credibility as a reliable partner in the Caribbean.

Furthermore, the intervention also had significant political implications. It served as a wake-up call for Caribbean nations to reassess their own political stability and security. The presence of U.S. military forces in Grenada highlighted the vulnerability of the region to external threats and the need for stronger regional cooperation in defense and security matters. This prompted the Caribbean nations to strengthen their own military capabilities and seek closer ties with other regional allies, such as Canada and the United Kingdom.

The intervention also had a lasting impact on regional stability. The United States' military operations in Grenada sent a clear message to other potential adversaries in the region, demonstrating the willingness of the United States to use force to protect its interests. This, in turn, contributed to a more stable security environment in the Caribbean, as it deterred potential threats and conflicts.

From a humanitarian perspective, the intervention brought attention to the dire socio-economic conditions in Grenada and the wider Caribbean. The United States, along with other international actors, provided aid and assistance to help rebuild Grenada's infrastructure and support its development. This humanitarian aspect of the intervention laid the groundwork for increased cooperation and engagement between the United States and the Caribbean in areas such as economic development, healthcare, and education.

In terms of intelligence agencies, the planning and execution of the intervention showcased the crucial role they play in shaping foreign policy decisions. The intelligence gathered by these agencies informed the decision-making process and highlighted the importance of accurate and timely information in military operations. This experience led to a greater emphasis on intelligence sharing and collaboration between the United States and its Caribbean partners, strengthening their overall cooperation in security matters.

Overall, the 1983 U.S. military intervention in Grenada had far-reaching implications for U.S.-Caribbean cooperation and engagement. It altered the political landscape, reshaped regional dynamics, and highlighted the importance of trust, stability, and intelligence collaboration in maintaining effective partnerships. Understanding these long-term implications is crucial for historians studying the intervention and its consequences on U.S.-Caribbean relations.